D0601700

PRISON PUPPIES

by Meish Goldish

Consultant: Gloria Gilbert Stoga
President and Founder, Puppies Behind Bars

PUBLISHING

New York, New York

Credits

Cover and Title Page, © Stephen Crowley/The New York Times/Redux; Cover TR, © James O'Connor; Cover CR, © Joyce Dopkeen/The New York Times/Redux; Cover BR, © Fabiano/Sipa/Newscom; TOC, © Altrendo Images/Getty Images; 4, © Joyce Dopkeen/The New York Times/Redux; 5, © Joyce Dopkeen/The New York Times/Redux; 6, © James O'Connor; 7, © Fabiano/Sipa/Newscom; 8, © Joyce Dopkeen/The New York Times/Redux; 9A, © Joyce Dopkeen/The New York Times/Redux; 9B, © Stephen Crowley/The New York Times/Redux; 10, © Radhika Chalasani/Redux; 11A, © AP Images/Daniel Hulshizer; 11B, © Fabiano/Sipa/Newscom; 12, © Radhika Chalasani/Redux; 13, © Stephen Crowley/The New York Times/Redux; 14, © AP Images/Ramin Talaie; 15, © Ambient Images Inc./SuperStock; 16, © Enrico Ferorelli; 17, © Andrew Holt/Alamy; 18, Courtesy of Domenica Campbell; 19, Courtesy of Domenica Campbell; 20, Courtesy of Domenica Campbell; 21, © Joyce Dopkeen/The New York Times/Redux; 22, © Fabiano/Sipa/Newscom; 23, Courtesy of Paul C Perricone N.Y.P.D. Bomb Squad; 24, © Elliot J. Sutherland/The Ottawa Herald; 25, Courtesy of Mike Parker; 26, © Fabiano/Sipa/Newscom; 27, © Fabiano/Sipa/Newscom; 29A, © Ben Molyneux Dogs/Alamy; 29B, © Fancy Collection/SuperStock; 29C, © Fotosearch/SuperStock.

Publisher: Kenn Goin
Creative Director: Spencer Brinker
Senior Editor: Lisa Wiseman
Design: Dawn Beard Creative
Photo Researcher: James O'Connor

Library of Congress Cataloging-in-Publication Data

Goldish, Meish.
  Prison puppies / by Meish Goldish.
    p. cm. — (Dog heroes)
  Includes bibliographical references and index.
  ISBN-13: 978-1-61772-151-9 (library binding)
  ISBN-10: 1-61772-151-4 (library binding)
  1. Service dogs—Juvenile literature. 2. Prisoners—Juvenile literature. I. Title.
  HV1569.6.G65 2011
  362.4'0483—dc22

                              2010037154

For more information, write to Bearport Publishing Company, Inc., 101 Fifth Avenue, Suite 6R, New York, New York 10003. Printed in the United States of America in North Mankato, Minnesota.

122010
10810CGD

10 9 8 7 6 5 4 3 2 1

Table of Contents

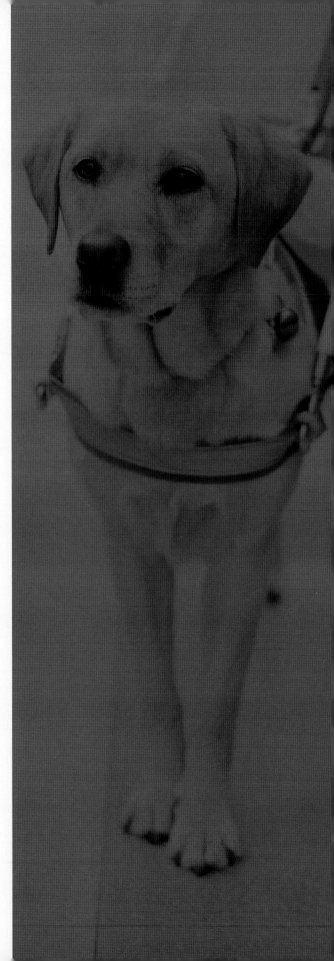

"Watch Me!"

A yellow Labrador retriever named Mitzie sat in a large room. Her **trainer**, Sharon, shouted a **command**. "Watch me!" she ordered the dog.

Quickly, Mitzie focused on Sharon's eyes. It was an important skill for Mitzie to learn. One day she might have a **disabled** owner who would only be able to use his or her eyes to give directions.

Sharon taught Mitzie to stare at her every time she said, "Watch me!"

Anyone watching Sharon work might think she's a **professional** dog trainer. In fact, she's an **inmate** in a New York State prison for women. She takes part in a program called Puppies Behind Bars (PBB), in which inmates raise puppies that later work as **service dogs** for people who are not in prison.

An inmate named Missy trains Portia, a yellow Labrador retriever, to close a door.

Inmates who train PBB dogs are called "puppy raisers." They get the puppies when the little dogs are about eight weeks old and raise them for about 18 months.

Starting Out

Puppies Behind Bars began in 1997. Gloria Gilbert Stoga, who worked for the mayor's office in New York City, started the program because she recognized that there were not enough people to train all the service dogs needed to help disabled people. Gloria had read about an Ohio prison where inmates raised **guide dogs** for the blind. She felt that a similar program could succeed in New York.

Gloria Gilbert Stoga with Fairfield (left) and Dudley (right)

Guide dogs for the blind are one type of service dog. Other kinds of service dogs are trained to help people with different disabilities, such as those who are unable to walk or hear.

Not everyone agreed with Gloria. Some prison **officials** worried that inmates might treat the dogs badly or teach them to attack prison guards. However, Gloria still managed to find a prison willing to test her idea. During the test phase, inmates raised five dogs for 18 months. Two of the **canines** became skilled enough to serve as guide dogs. Gloria proved that the PBB program could work.

Gloria Gilbert Stoga (right) started the Puppies Behind Bars program at the Bedford Hills Correctional Facility in New York State. Today, PBB operates in six prisons—three for men and three for women—in New York, New Jersey, and Connecticut.

Teaching the Teachers

As the head of PBB, Gloria teaches inmates how to train their puppies. Every week, she and other dog trainers give a six-hour class in each prison. They show the puppy raisers how to teach the commands, 90 in all, that the animals must learn in order to succeed as service dogs. One inmate even had to learn to give the commands in French. The dog she was training was eventually going to work in France.

Puppy raiser Tracy is teaching her dog, Holly, how to help a person in a wheelchair.

Inmates start with basic commands such as "heel" and "sit." They use treats as a reward when the dog performs the right action. Since their puppies will work as service dogs, the puppy raisers also teach them how to do everyday tasks such as pulling open doors, turning lights on and off—and even getting bottles from the refrigerator.

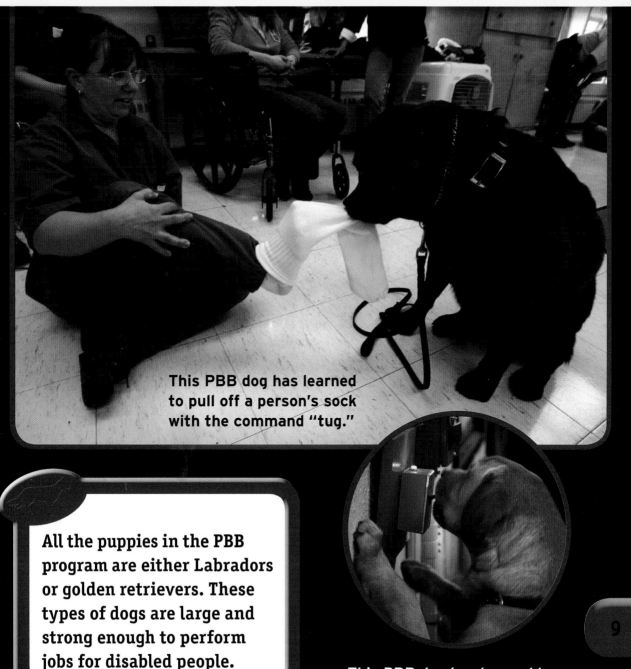

This PBB dog has learned to pull off a person's sock with the command "tug."

All the puppies in the PBB program are either Labradors or golden retrievers. These types of dogs are large and strong enough to perform jobs for disabled people.

This PBB dog has learned how to turn a light switch on.

Perfect Partners

While inmates teach their puppies, the puppies also teach them. How? The inmates learn to be patient with their animals. They also learn to be responsible for someone besides themselves. One puppy raiser named Kareem said that before he joined the PBB program, his life was "all about me." By raising his puppy Tucket, Kareem learned to put someone else's needs before his own.

Kareem learned how to be more responsible by taking care of Tucket.

Inmates also learn to work as a team with their puppies. Usually, the pair make excellent partners. The dogs don't judge the puppy raisers on the past crimes that landed them in prison. The animals just want to be cared for and loved. In return, they show the inmates love and **loyalty**.

As they train their dogs, inmates learn to cooperate with the animals as well as with other puppy raisers.

Puppy raisers in the PBB program not only attend training classes, they also must complete reading assignments, do homework, and pass written tests in order to stay in the program.

Always There

Training a PBB puppy is a full-time job. In the morning, inmates feed their dogs and then exercise them as a group. In one exercise, a puppy raiser walks his or her dog around a **courtyard**. Another inmate throws a basketball in their path. The dog learns to stay with its puppy raiser and not be **distracted** by the ball.

An inmate teaches a pup not to respond to distractions as balls are thrown around during a PBB training class.

Puppy raisers spend the whole day with their dogs, even taking them to work. The inmates have jobs within the prison, such as working in the library, the laundry room, or barber shop. Bringing the pups to work allows the animals to get used to a busy **environment** with many people.

At night, each puppy stays in its puppy raiser's cell. The dog sleeps in a dog crate near the puppy raiser's bed.

At night, the puppies stay with the puppy raisers in their cells.

During the week, the only time that inmates and their puppies are not together is when the inmates eat their meals. Prison rules do not allow dogs in the cafeteria.

Outside Visits

Inmates spend a lot of time with their puppies, but sometimes the dogs get to leave the prison. Usually a couple of times a week, PBB **volunteers** take the dogs to their homes to get them used to things they don't experience in prison, such as riding in a car or hearing a telephone ring. It's all part of the puppy's training to become a service dog.

When outside the prison, some PBB dogs wear vests to let people know that they are part of the Puppies Behind Bars program.

As part of their training, dogs in the PBB program get to experience life outside of prison. Here, a volunteer takes Potter, a five-month-old Labrador retriever, for a walk in a mall.

Some **cadets** at the United States Military Academy at West Point, New York, also volunteer to take care of the puppies outside of the prison. The PBB staff brings the dogs to their school. There, the cadets pair off with the puppies for several hours. Sometimes the dogs spend part of the time visiting wounded soldiers at West Point's hospital. It helps the animals learn to be around disabled people.

The United States Military Academy at West Point, New York, is a school that trains men and women to become officers in the U.S. Army.

At West Point, shown here, PBB dogs get used to seeing other kinds of uniforms besides those worn in prison.

Leading the Way

The puppy raisers and volunteers help prepare PBB dogs for specific jobs. When the program began, the first puppies were trained only to become guide dogs. One such dog was Victoria, a black Labrador retriever. As part of her training, a puppy raiser named Mercedes taught Victoria basic commands such as "stay" and "come." Victoria also learned how to alert her human partner to danger. This is especially important for dogs working with blind people who rely on the dogs to get around.

Mercedes and other inmates share the experience of being guided by Victoria while blindfolded.

After Victoria was fully trained, she went to work for a blind man named Willi Richards. The dog changed Richards's life. "Before Victoria, I was a prisoner in my own house," he said. Through Mercedes's hard work, however, she has given Richards the freedom to get around.

Guide dogs help their blind owners get around safely

Depending on what kind of work they're going to do, most PBB dogs start working as service dogs as soon as they complete their prison training.

A New Job

As the PBB program grew, its puppies were trained to help other disabled people besides the blind. In 2006, inmates began to raise dogs for wounded American war **veterans** who had served in Iraq or Afghanistan. The new program was called Dog Tags: Service Dogs for Those Who've Served Us. The first PBB dog raised for a war veteran was Pax, a yellow Labrador retriever.

Pax was the first graduate of the Dog Tags program.

Puppy raiser Laurie trained Pax for Sergeant (Sgt.) Bill Campbell, who had fought in Iraq and now suffered from post-traumatic stress disorder, or PTSD. Sergeant Campbell refused to leave his house, afraid he would be attacked by strangers. Could Pax help him deal with his fears?

Sergeant Campbell in Iraq

Post-traumatic stress disorder is an illness that causes a person to feel very afraid, nervous, and sad. The person may suffer from nightmares, a fear of public places, and loss of memory.

Making a Difference

After receiving his dog, Sergeant Campbell still didn't want to leave his house at first. However, Pax forced him to. "He has to go for walks," Sergeant Campbell explained.

Today, Sergeant Campbell copes with his PTSD much better because of Pax. The dog is trained to alert his owner if a stranger approaches. To do so, Pax stands between Sergeant Campbell and the person to keep them separated.

Sergeant Campbell feels much safer knowing that Pax will prevent strangers from approaching him.

Besides Sergeant Campbell, Pax has helped another person—Laurie, the inmate who raised him. Through her work with Pax, Laurie has been able to give a war veteran his freedom after she lost her own freedom as an inmate. She said, "What I've done is put a year of love into this puppy, who in turn will give a lifetime of love to Bill and his wife."

Sergeant Campbell visited the Bedford Hills prison to thank Laurie for raising Pax.

Pax usually wears a special vest that tells strangers not to pet him, since it could distract him while he's helping Sergeant Campbell.

The Nose Knows

Not all PBB puppies are raised to serve disabled people. Sheeba, a yellow Labrador retriever, was trained to sniff for bombs. After America was attacked by a terrorist group on September 11, 2001, the demand for bomb-sniffing dogs grew. PBB now works with bomb experts from the New York City Police Department (NYPD) to raise prison puppies for the job.

Bomb-sniffing dogs can smell a bomb even if it is hidden inside a package.

For Sheeba's training, her puppy raiser Shakirah hid a special toy around a room. Then Shakirah encouraged Sheeba to use her super sense of smell to sniff out the hidden item. They did this over and over again until Sheeba learned to rely on her nose to find the toy. After Sheeba was fully trained, she went to work for the NYPD. A bomb expert at the police department, Paul Perricone, became her **handler**.

Paul Perricone and Sheeba

Dogs have an amazing sense of smell. They smell odors about one million times better than humans do. Bomb-sniffing dogs are trained to recognize the odors of all the chemicals that may be used to make a bomb.

Together Again

After spending so much time with the puppies, the inmates grow to love them. So it's always sad to have to part with them after their training has been completed. Roberto, an inmate at a prison in Fishkill, New York, raised a yellow Labrador retriever named Frankie. The day the dog left prison, Roberto said, "It was hard for me to realize that the next morning I was going to wake up and not actually feed her."

Frankie

Luckily, Roberto and Frankie managed to have a **reunion** a few months later. Sgt. Allen Hill, a war veteran with PTSD who received Frankie as a service dog, visited Roberto in prison and brought along Frankie. When the dog saw her former trainer, she ran straight toward him.

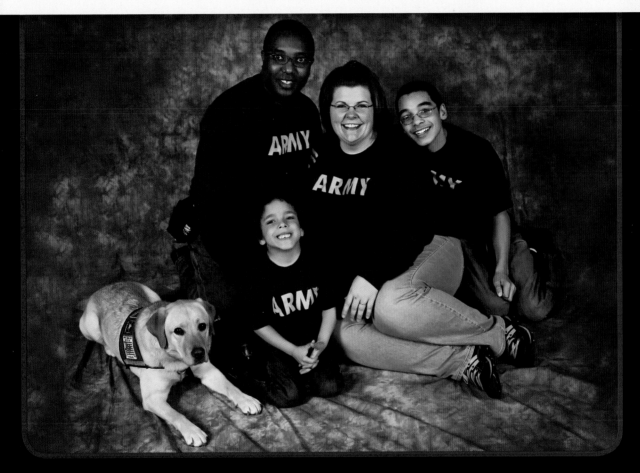

Sergeant Hill, his family, and Frankie

Though it doesn't happen very often, some inmates have reunions with the dogs. The meetings allow the puppy raiser and the dog's new owner to share information and stories about the animal.

Good Deeds

Puppies Behind Bars has accomplished a lot since the program began in 1997. Inmates have trained more than 600 dogs. Many of the animals now work as service dogs for disabled people, including blind people and veterans. More than half of the PBB dogs work as bomb sniffers.

Puppies Behind Bars is just one of many prison programs in the United States where inmates raise puppies for disabled people. Other programs are currently running in more than 20 states across the country.

Today, about 125 inmates take part in the Puppies Behind Bars program.

PBB has proven valuable in many ways. The dogs **benefit** more than just the people they serve. They also help the people who raised them. They allow the inmates, who are locked behind bars, to contribute to **society** in a positive way. These dogs have proven that they truly are a man's—or woman's—best friend!

Eighteen months of dog training in prison can lead to a lifetime of joy for a disabled person.

Just the Facts

- Before inmates can take part in the Puppies Behind Bars program, they must have a good behavior record in prison for two years. They also must be recommended by prison officials as being honest and dependable.

- The puppy raisers keep an ongoing journal with notes about their dogs' habits and behavior. Later, the journals are given to the people the dogs will serve, so that the owners can better work with their animals.

- War veterans who are to receive service dogs from PBB go through a two-week training session with PBB instructors in order to learn how to work with their dogs.

- Most of the puppies for the PBB program are purchased from professional dog **breeders** who raise Labradors and golden retrievers. PBB has its own small breeding program as well.

- It costs about $26,000 to raise and train each dog in the PBB program. The money pays for the puppies, staff trainers, dog supplies, class materials, and travel expenses. The inmates, however, are not paid for their work.

- The entire cost of the PBB program is paid for by **donations** from businesses and private individuals. The people who receive the service dogs pay nothing.

Common Breeds: PRISON PUPPIES

yellow Labrador retriever

black Labrador retriever

golden retriever

29

benefit (BEN-uh-fit) to help or be helped in some way

breeders (BREE-durz) people who raise selected types of dogs in order for them to give birth to puppies with specific qualities

cadets (kuh-DETS) people who are training to become members of the armed forces or a police force

canines (KAY-ninez) members of the dog family

command (kuh-MAND) an order given to a person or animal

courtyard (KORT-*yard*) an open area surrounded by walls

disabled (diss-AY-buhld) unable to do certain things because of an illness or injury

distracted (dis-TRAKT-id) having one's attention drawn away by something

donations (doh-NAY-shuhnz) gifts of money or supplies to help people in need

environment (en-VYE-ruhn-muhnt) the area and conditions that surround one

guide dogs (GIDE DAWGZ) dogs that are trained to lead blind people

handler (HAND-lur) a person who trains and manages an animal such as a dog

inmate (IN-mayt) someone who has been sentenced to live in a prison

loyalty (LOI-uhl-tee) faithfulness to someone or something, such as one's country

officials (uh-FISH-uhlz) people who hold important positions in an organization

professional (pruh-FESH-uh-nuhl) a person who gets paid to do something as a job rather than just for fun

reunion (ree-YOON-yuhn) a meeting between animals or people who have not seen one another for a long time

service dogs (SUR-viss DAWGZ) dogs that are trained to help people who are disabled in some way

society (suh-SYE-uh-tee) all the people who live in the same country or area and share the same laws and customs

trainer (TRAY-nur) a person who teaches an animal to behave in a certain way

veterans (VET-ur-uhnz) people who have served in the armed forces

volunteers (*vol*-uhn-TIHRZ) people who offer to do a job without pay

Bibliography

Davis, Kathy Diamond. *Therapy Dogs: Training Your Dog to Reach Others.* Wenatchee, WA: Dogwise (2002).

Davis, Marci, and Melissa Bunnell. *Working Like Dogs: The Service Dog Guidebook.* Crawford, CO: Alpine Publications (2007).

Solberg, Paul. *Puppies Behind Bars: Training Puppies to Change Lives.* New York: Glitterati (2007).

Stevens, Debi. *Prison-Trained Dogs: An Inside Job with Community Wide Rewards.* Denver: Colorado Correctional Industries Print Shop (2007).

Read More

McDaniel, Melissa. *Guide Dogs.* New York: Bearport (2005).

Ruffin, Frances E. *Police Dogs.* New York: Bearport (2005).

Tagliaferro, Linda. *Service Dogs.* New York: Bearport (2005).

Tagliaferro, Linda. *Therapy Dogs.* New York: Bearport (2005).

Learn More Online

Visit these Web sites to learn more about Puppies Behind Bars as well as other prison puppy programs:

abcnews.go.com/Health/MindMoodNews/story?id=4476070&page=1

www.docs.state.ny.us/NewsRoom/external_news/2008-06-01_Prison_Puppies.pdf

www.puppiesbehindbars.com

www.time.com/time/photogallery/0,29307,1911990_1913005,00.html

www.usatoday.com/NEWS/usaedition/2009-11-11-puppies11_ST_U.htm

Index

About the Author

Meish Goldish has written more than 200 books for children. His books *Bug-a-licious* and *Michael Phelps: Anything Is Possible* were Children's Choices Reading List Selections in 2010. He lives in Brooklyn, New York.